ANTHROPOLOGICAL STUDY

Anthropological Study

Lauren Miller

QUERENCIA

Querencia Press – Chicago IL

QUERENCIA PRESS

ISBN 978 1 963943 05 4

www.querenciapress.com

First Published in 2025

Querencia Press, LLC
Chicago IL

Printed & Bound in the United States of America

CONTENTS

I

I wanted to walk straight on through the red grass and over the edge of the world, which could not be very far away.

—*Willa Cather*

House-Sitting

Welcome home, love

The foundation crumbled while you were gone

I can't remember if it was me
or the hurricane

I stopped caring
after the third cigar

The rabbit is stuck in the spice cabinet

Your brother called twice
so I gave him our duvet

The Ekpyrotic Universe Theory

if i hadn't been a girl whose knuckles turned violet instead of white,
like polar bears traced with lemon juice fingers onto printer paper

when i held a raw calf liver over a cast iron skillet with onions
coughing up cooking spray and could still smell the undigested
sedative leaking on the inside of the organ

i think we would have been more inclined to notice that when we
opened one another's mouths with our own hot breathing

containing sapphic dark-matter spilled out into celestial oblivion

an oblivion where girls kissing girls is akin to emptying our world
of artists who try to make reverse graffiti a thing and the softest
hairs on the bloomed terrain of her harvest moon belly are made of
ultraviolet light that feels like an electric blanket on the highest
setting

and i see how when my hand touches her collarbone

a teenage mother composed of ancient starstuff births heavenly
bodies, and when the heart hanging beneath her sun-stale skin beats
against my chest

that is the time in which a cosmic alchemist melts gobs of
luminescence and we have both made exoplanets out of lesbian sex

Spring Comes With Too Much Bounty

If no one was around

I really think
she would morph into a

hydrangea bloom
for all the times that
she's made my eyes water

Maybe not in totality

Perhaps
just the petals
budding baby blue
from the cracks
in the skin around
her fingertips

Or the roots
breaking through
ceiling plaster
and winding around
the electrical wires in the walls

Just the earth
sown with her fertilized atoms

If I found her
as a hydrangea
I would collect her in my harvest
of nice flora

and shut her
inside works of literature
whose authors

have
forsaken their genius

and when she was dead

I would keep her remains
on my tea table
for days that are
stupid with desirability

Insect Courtship

Last week
I thought
I was
aging into a firefly
but it turns out
the gleam
was just
audacity
laden with chamomile
so today
I continue to
acquaint my vision
with the dark

soon
it won't be as bleary
and my hands
will lose
their fear of
touching without knowing
if the touch will bruise

Ballet Before Kissing

A referendum has occurred
and now I sit here

the hair on my legs making music
offering my atonement
for baking your vintage alarm clock
into a raspberry cake
and eating it whole

It was just
that I wanted to see you

do a carousel twirl

out of your blush chiffon
one last time
before I went

Don't go too high or else you'll fall and falling hurts

A persimmon tree which grows fruit from the sound of fizzing soda

I like that tree

Four times a day, I pray for its safety in this potent, lovely wildness

Bubble Bath

Laid flat in the dishwasher today

let the soap get in my eyes

broke all the plates beneath the pleats of my stomach

Then I wept for six or seven hours
and threw away all my blinds

so that my body can get used to being seen
and my arms will stop harboring my skin
in their ashamed embrace
when my girlfriend wants to take a bath
without a layer of foam suds hiding our nakedness

the water
being the only thing we touch
with any sort of sexual implication

Melted Gelato Soup

I am perturbed
this evening
by the evidence against Darwinism
that has arrived

in the form
of her fuchsia hair dye
ascending to

champagne hues
after we stood
for two hours in hellish shower
water
that singed each time
it fell
onto exposed skin

so she says,
"Charles Darwin was a fascist,"

and

"The hairdresser went too dark, anyways."

And then
with our heads wetting
our rattiest pillowcases
and pink seeping into faux organic cotton

We watch a nature documentary
and
we pretend that homophobia
is a similar experience

to still-spotted deer mothers
refusing to nurse their unviable fawns

The Funeral for My Snowman Will Be Held Before We Lose
Our Conviction

I don't want to die today

and I don't want to stop being in love with you
and with this winter
so I ask you to watch *Casablanca* with me.

Your hair smells like powdered sugar
and we've been in pajamas all day.

Yours have little buttons on them that I think would be
relatively easy to undo.

Being trapped inside my body is less of an affliction right now
because I'm holding your face in my frostbitten hands
and there is ice on the road outside
so everything is quiet.

I want
to make
a snow angel

The Centennial Lightbulb

I don't know

how to be
smaller

more like the seed
than the bloom

less loud
and
less gaudy

I want to be contained

and inconsequential

a spoonful

and not the whole bowl
because

I no longer see the point
of being thirsty

and I've started to be able to stomach tap water.

Maybe now
I will find a lover
who is out of the closet

and won't hold my hand
like it is a dead worm but
a
type of chrysanthemum.

I can
learn to
be worth looking at

maybe

a pearl of some kind?

Nicotine Patch

I am trying to be less cynical since I quit doing heroin forty-nine
days before this one

I had to crawl into a nectarine pit
to keep myself from
cracking open
while at last facing ramification for my sins

Which looked like me
waiting to become numb from the rime within my bones

vomiting up every iota of exultation
for a chance at salvation
and

being reduced to the salt in my sweat

After I had been fully withdrawn
from the craving for
viability to
be gratifying

I found an Art Nouveau exhibit at a museum in downtown Seattle
and pressed the moon surface on
my thumb against every
piece of artwork
until security escorted me back onto the filthy sidewalk

The following morning
I walked across a church altar
with mud on my bare feet

This evening I did not touch my lips
to the Siddur
before I tucked it away

I am not a good person

but I no longer only ache
to have a needle in my arm

That's something
at least

Canonized

I leave my window stretched, as open

as the seconds before a child
realizes she is person
and not a plum waiting to turn sugary
enough for her mother
to let her sleep swaddled by her insides again

I do this
so damp things can spill
into the parts
where I have been hollowed out
and hallowed

I was not created
to be the silence around an empty church
after it's been desecrated
and the core is no longer blessed

I am only the keeper
of ill saints
because she offered first

Lazy Suppers

If acting as if adding shredded mozzarella to microwaved
frozen pizza makes the taste better is a proper example
of the abnegation that I possess
over not being born an affluent French spinster's sphinx cat
then I guess I have something to tell the girl who kisses
my stomach under the winter-spoiled indigo of my bedroom
on nights where monogamy seems plausible

The Teenage Angst of Being Twenty-Two and Alone

This nose ring is itching as I make sad art

I'm getting anxious again

That famous woman died recently

I saw it on the news

damn it all to hell

how badly I want to be remembered
for the way that I catch rain
in my rainboots
so that when I wear them
the heaviness in my step has a purpose

beyond that I want people to hear me coming

or for how I fuck women

because fucking women makes sense

women
are the only soft parts in all this jagged edge

Non-Lucidity

I dreamt under pulsing lamplight of being carbon monoxide's mistress, and oh, how glorious the nullity of asphyxiation was.

emphasized text

My polite resistance to being a bitch
is wearing thin, like the line between
a literature professor and someone who
sill reads physical copies of *The New York
Times*, so I've decided to get a minimalist
tattoo of a rhinoceros on my wrist, and this
evening I will drink inexhaustible cups of
black coffee after consuming cacio e pepe
from a bowl whose innards are stained an
inky hue of mauve from an attempt at
homemade blackberry jam which arose when
my life was still governed by untreated
agoraphobia

[insert secularist diatribe here]

the rosehip perfume
was my undoing

I say the rosary while kneeling in a public restroom stall with a
broken lock

Freedom Like a Displaced Universe

Left my domesticity
at the dollar store

Heard it sold quickly

It was the last carton
of midsummer-warmed blackberries
before briar overtakes them
as the numbing season descends

Nonalignment
has become
my
raw condition

Words
are playthings
without reason

The language
frothing in my chest
is comprised
of satisfying sounds

rippling hummingbird wings

blood sweeping through veins
when a hand is pressed to an ear

dried out meadows beneath horizon arms

I've made virgins
from wildflowers

They touch

my face at night
with such softness
it provokes me

The tenderest one
is to be my bride

She shares my pillow

Untamed
winds
don't

dare
to pleasure themselves with my tresses

I am sustained
by will alone

Manna is not needed here

I draw out its milk for butter

My aliveness
is more alive than yours

II

I believe in God, but not as one thing, not as an old man in the sky. I believe that what people call God is something inside all of us.

—*John Lennon*

Palpable Elegies

Dust in
daybreak warm light
makes things sacred

The river inside the hibiscus
where Moses was
set adrift by a mother
who was the true deliverer

Nectarine sap spilling down children's arms

A honeyed sonnet

houses with creaky stairs

foxholes and
azure thread

the language of trees

Sacred things
that are not graveyards—

because those
are not
sacred

they are

overgrown with grief
that brims
as vermouth does
when poured into stout pitchers
by a mourner—

are besmirched from soil
disordered by ghosts
attempting to separate
paradise
from inferno

are emptied
even
when bursting

Sanction must be deserved

Wasted

Imbibing grapefruit tonic atop a frozen-over pond
while somewhere else two people
are forgetting each other's favorite movies

to see how long it takes to be
swallowed
by cold things

This isn't scintillating enough

Atlas is a Woman

Perhaps it is the daughters
who hold up the promised land
and keep it placid with their
open hands

the tips of their fingers are iris bulbs

The Derivation

What often gets lost
in the marring of the girl

is that

man

is only a small component
of
Femaninity

and it's spoken so quickly
it has become

the most habitual malapropism
in our language

We spell it

Femininity
in an attempt
to erase the man
from anything
owned by a woman
because to have femininity
is to be lesser
but the word

is still the word
and it is meant to hold an
a
bound in its nucleus

With what was but one of Adam's ribs
the lord sculpted a mother
for the entirety of his scion

Matcha Croissant

A little sister
sucks on

fleshy saliva

from where baby teeth were
stillborn in her mouth

and this girl
who will someday be an
absurdist author

she pinches
a thumb and middle finger
that are not yet plump
from overuse
into
the puff pastry
still
dripping
off the counter
like

a tangelo

rotting

in

Independence Day heat

Becomings

Half slow and half fast is how girls grow into women. Some of them become ladies, their bones lacy and easily splintered, like secrets known by more than one mind. All of them have softness at the meeting of their canines. A few will spit it out along with burnt garlic cloves from the lining of their stomachs. There is a solstice in the jaw of each woman and she gets to choose the sun that it obeys.

Value Creation

Female Orgasms

Infidelity

A paramour was made
out of the garnet hair
that still clung to her polyester bedsheets
after laundry day

It will probably be
iconography
by next week

For now it is
artsy pornography
and,

sadly,
a very poor
affair partner

aisling

kissing a philosophy major
is only worth a discussion
about who is the ultimate
beneficiary of moral action
if they know how to correctly pronounce
the Irish word
suaimhneas
because it makes their tongue
taste like comice pears

It's Sad and It's Sweet

Listening to
experimental song refrains
in an ivory Volkswagen Beetle
with erratic heat
past bedtime
at a red light

in sleet

Flu Season

Apathy to an
accountant
is standard operating

a symptom of enjoying mathematics
and

abundances that wouldn't matter
to the paper clip
if they were given sentience

Apathy to a poet
is a sign of illness

because the minute
a poet ceases to find magnificence
in

the way rain sounds
when it hits a bucket filled with drops
already fallen

as though they are not siblings
from the same set of condensated parents

that is when they have made a shelter

out of a brown bear carcass

while they try in vain to recall
in which direction home lies

A Sinking

A soup spoon
rests
at the

far end
of the community pool

boys and girls
who are little sages
with cerise eyes
deem it unworthy
of hoarding

The spoon
is a
talisman

it will not
stir

Female

Standing in the center of a sagging roof

how splendid
how incredible

how utterly ridiculous

god or goddess or person or bird
they'll never know which

When it collapses

there will be chaos
and that is the stuff we anguish for
as women
built from ember
then told not to burn

until the witch hunt is complete

The Childhood Artwork Kept by Mothers

We paint hideously
with our fingers
when we are

without a brush

or a sponge
heavy
with chartreuse

because we want to leave
something
more permanent
than

children
or

paperbacks

and the only things
a person can make
using solely themselves

are an orgasm

and a fat pointillism landscape
that they keep
under a bed
or inside
the linen closet that is never opened

because we have all agreed
to only show other bodies
filled with blood that surges

things that maintain
the fallacy
that is
humanity being exquisite
rather than
a damned bastard malformation
of the cosmos

David and Bathsheba

A lesson

in the force
of a ravishing naked woman

III

She made no apologies for her wild heart.

—Michele Rose Gilman

Fucked Up Gender Identity

She is a girl

because she is not anything else

Not a pill
to be taken every morning
in suppression of something unwanted

Not a housecat
lazy
because it's never known starvation pains
or the feel of something
that hasn't been touched by anyone else before

Not the clouds
for which stagnancy is outlawed

Not an appendix

useless
and grotesque

and carried around
so that we have a portion of our younger selves
still there
as a relic

after we've been given grace
for not knowing
something we should have
for the last time

To be a girl
all you need
is practice

churning anger into ice cream

that still tastes delectable
even though it
is laced with bleach
to purify
rotting flesh
before the sacrifice

The Old Brag of My Heart

She sinks
into
a glass of raw milk
with the dairy
having evolved
into a kind of
film that
cherishes the hemangioma
on the nape
of Her neck

that an unwashed clairvoyant
on the Atlantic City
boardwalk
said was evidence of
reincarnation

and She holds Her breath
cornered inside Her ribcage
where it
decomposes
into
a motif for
the literary malnourishment
of the hipster intellectual
with an

art history degree
from liberal arts college

Autobiography

Her name has a phonetically incorrect "y" where there should be an "e" and because of that she never learned how to sound out unfamiliar words. When people read her name they think her socioeconomic status is lower than it is, which is classist and rooted in racism against things that could be labeled as Black culture, but she is white so whatever. She keeps her veiled chameleon in a twenty-gallon fish tank below her bedroom window, despite the guy at the pet store telling her not to do that. She has been vegetarian since she was eleven but when alone she lusts to lick boiled lamb blood from a pool in her hands. This is probably because when she was little her father used to make her help him scrape the skin from venison meat before they ate it. She holds her piss until she gets bladder infections because she doesn't like the sound of her pee hitting the toilet water and one time she told her mom that and her mom told her to stop saying every thought she had out loud and nice girls don't talk about anything that is expelled from their holes. Losing her virginity was the only time she ever felt loved because consenting to a loss makes the losing feel different. Sometimes in the morning she is sad she woke up still breathing but the time when you've died but aren't fully dead yet seems like it would hurt too much.

Ashy

Her dried-out skin
asks her why
she doesn't use lotion
when she could smell like eucalyptus
and prevent
earthquakes
that pit body against bone
and she says
that
the sun will still
eventually
break bread with Orion
and devour the Earth
despite the state of
her epidermis

Late to Everything and Also Iodine Deficient

She often says
dirty things
to her vanity
mirror
such as

"I'm wearing a bra today."

Her lips
have an intrinsically
blue tint

Sometimes
it's tolerable

Those are the times when she wants a reminder
that even though she is alive
she is still
on her way
to dying

That makes her feel close
to the tortoise
she had when she was six

which was murdered by the family dog
after she left it out in
the backyard
for a bit of non-synthetic light

but her older sister didn't know
so she let the dog go outside

Other times
the cobalt

is instead
the origin

for her animosity of womanhood

Those are the times when
she layers on coal
like it's black lipstick

it looks ugly
but it does the job

She regularly
abandons library books
on public transit
because paying the fine
means she gets to talk
to the nice lady
who works the public library's front desk on Wednesdays

Her favorite kind of coffee
has eleven pumps of pumpkin spice
but when it is her turn to order
she always ends up getting
a plain
and adds her own sweetener

This person
sort of wishes she
had a driver's license

And a toaster that worked

A nightgown with little daisies on it

The ability to stop
disassociating
all the time

Her greatest achievement being a fairly intact psyche

Exile appears funny to her

A really good joke
like carrying around a piece of dead tortoise
in her dress pocket

Performative Witchcraft

the Leo is in full moon
so she lights a peony
candle in a silent film
matinee because she
wants to get drunk tonight
and start an argument
with her partner about
whose turn it is to pick a
movie to stream in the background
during the weekends spent
holding space for their
bodies to learn where
each other is most
sensitive to gnawing

Leonard Cohen

poetry was born to create temple
for the hallelujahs
tethered
to her empty skin beneath a humbled night

Skinny Dipping

Her half moons
fill with molasses
when her
lilt is slowed by unrest

Look,
she calls,

the soft arch of her breasts
brushing the river's surface
as she faces Altair

the soul of her eyelids

distempered with ruby
from its light

Look,

I am the color of old stars

And that she was

Standing in the stream
nude

ankles
submerged in mire

Cicadas
a patronage
quieted by the hot
breeze working
into

her sopping hair

Lore

was later told
about how the world
stopped turning

so that she could
steady herself in the
water

It was
of course

a contorted reminiscence

but
how lovely
a thought

getting a gnat in your eye

Maybe
it will be better in
August

the only time she remembers her personhood is when she chews up
wet soap

#10

Her hamartia was so pretty as it materialized inside the creative
nonfiction of a Walmart parking lot

#11

Today she let me carry her wet socks and they felt like slippery herring in the back of a throat and I think we are nearing viola crescendos of nightly intimacy

#12

She puts too much salt in her gazpacho but I gladly let the soup sink into my stomach because it's a very romantic meal to share on a rickety fifth-floor terrace

Hosanna. Hosanna, Hosanna

Her fingernails
are salmon skin silverish
so that
when she scratches devils
into the wallpaper
as she sits on the cold of her bathroom floor
naked
and wet
and starving for the crumbs
from thick pieces of brioche
slathered in apple butter
that she swept underneath the counter
fifty-seven minutes ago

the silver paint
flakes off into the hair on her unclothed thigh
and she glimmers
for a little while

Her walls are uneven
with woman-made grooves
a sea
that never settles

an infant who asks for wine
but is only allowed the breast

She cradles nice words
in the folds of her hair
so she can furnish unpolished silences

Her doctor said
she needed to drink more calcium
so she started leaving figs on the
sill of her window

and eats their withered meat
for every meal

A houseless crow
follows her around when she walks to
find hazelnuts in the park
because he thinks she is a carcass

Some afternoons she is one
but her body
nonetheless
conserves an agreeable
rosy aroma

and the ceaseless thwack of her pulse
worries each of them

there is a beautiful part, but this isn't it

She smokes

because there is glory
in contributing to her own demise

It's not that she doesn't want to be alive

She does

She thinks she does

but
what is an existence without glory?

It is a nonexistence

A sort of
bardo
for the blurry-eyed

It washes the dust from in between eyelashes

but she
doesn't want to see
her succumbing place

It's ugly
a nothing that she fills with smoke and ash
until she can't discern
her own non-gloriousness
from the gray

Because it is not divine
to be her own death

not when the death
sets her on fire
sets her on fire

sets her on fire

sets her on fire

What she likes about cigarettes
are the matches used to light them

No one ever told her
not to play with matches

nor make a friend out of flame

She tells herself now
that the grandeur of burning
is a delusion

but she doesn't believe it

Lies are inhaled
with the fumes

But
once more:

there is no glory in the blaze

Hell is meant for the afterlife

leave it be

leave it be

she smokes without a reason
and that is the reason

Wedding

over and over and over again

she hears a calling
from the
entrails
of a timber wolf

the canid remembers
the thinness
of her step
and he does not scare
when she approaches

her georgette dresses
are lacerated
each and every one

from when she
climbs into

the wolf's putrid mouth

his heartbeat
bashes her eardrum

deafness now looms

woman and beast
often
bellow together
even if their howls
are only met by
empty
witching hour
skies

soon woman will butcher wolf
for meat
or wisdom

that is the way of things

trees have borne witness to it

over and over and over again

that is the way of things

Omelette

She was cracked open
by god

she spilled out onto the floor
oozed
took up so much damned space
that there wasn't a step

one could take
without getting yolk
poured into the crevices
between their toes

her shell was mashed
inside a closed drawer fist
because it had been too ugly

and how dare
a woman be anything
other than pleasing to look at

how dare she have something
on the inside
that made a mess when it was finally allowed out

she was too dangerous for consumption

eat her
and be damned

and people
would be damned

because
they are not accustomed

to the act
of leaving eggs undisturbed
in the carton

every single one
at some point
meets the bottom
of a seething stomach

broken
and used up
and ugly
because they don't have to be pretty anymore

Bread and Butter

Sourdough starter
is without mercy

akin to a young boy
who lobs smooth-faced stones
at chickadees in flight
so that he is able to feel Herculean

The boy will remember that feeling
when he becomes a man

His grandmother hopes
he masters the art
of self-restraint

before she has to look up
to meet his eyes

A fermented culture
comprised of newborn flour
and ancient water
is the same

Except it is a girl
and girls without mercy
become

mothers
who shouldn't have children
but do

Or

worse

they become mothers
who shouldn't have a baby
and don't

These mothers
make heirs out of
shattered obsidian

Their hands have
more exposed flesh
than intact

Let the sourdough
finish
before
it begins

or let it burn in the oven

I don't care

just put it out of its torment
before that's what it breeds

See you next year

Permanently seventeen and over it, and
singing Etta James from her diaphragm,
not her throat, while she outlines a rosemary
sprig on my shoulder with one trembling hand
holding a knitting needle saturated in the ink from
a blue pen. Her hair is platinum blonde
with the brown peeking out as her roots
emerge. We are buzzed and more than a little
of the stupor is demanded by our youth
rather than the hard strawberry lemonade we
pillaged from her eldest sister. Earlier she
had a date with a boy who called her
"interesting" and his goodbye kiss is making
her question her sexuality. I am overwhelmed
by the devotion that I have for her in the
flush of that summer night in her basement,
and this is how I choose to remember her. The
only vestige of her that I've kept is the Backstreet
Boys t-shirt I wear to bed. My dad keeps asking
if the reason I'm still crying is because I was
in love with her—and I was, just not in the way
he thinks. On Tuesday I moved into the townhouse.
It's fine, but she isn't worn into its bends.
Everyone says her echo is enough but they are liars.

Slut Shaming

The genesis
of her villainism
was when she went to
the pharmacy with a leaking cold sore
in the corner of her bottom lip
and a holier-than-thou
grandmother
glanced at her
then
gave her preteen granddaughter
an impromptu sermon
under her breath
about
promiscuity
Colossians 3:5
and how men won't buy cattle
when the milk is already free
so the drugstore skank
followed them into the
hair care product aisle
and inquired
whether they knew where the
lube was kept in the store
then bought two jars
of the cotton candy-flavored kind
and declined a bag
at checkout
then drove home
and had
frenzied oral sex
with a nonbinary person
she met at a dingy club
and has no intention
of marrying

Burial Grounds

Her baptism
was done by the sea
and it blamed
a restless sky that had deepened its waters
with rainfall
when she drowned during the christening

She was Catholic
and Catholics don't get baptized in the ocean
but she was already gray-haired

and her tongue
had tasted death's brine before

they were acquaintances
soon to be lovers

and she needed to be owned
by something
before they consummated the relationship

She chose God
to be her shepherd
even though
she was no fucking sheep

she just admired
the way he'd taught the tides

to be faithful husbands
to the shore

and bring their quartz wives
jewelry
each time they came home to them

Death was a gentle lover

he waited until she couldn't hear him
before he took her

she'd thought he was an unruly wave
when he kissed her
a little too hard
in the green waters

and he swallowed her
before she could think anything more

It was better that way

her lungs didn't have time
to miss the taste of air
before oxygen wasn't needed any longer

It Doesn't Matter Why

She goes to the creek without
her glasses on

and grasps anything that fits into
her redbud blossom palms

When she gets home
she places everything she filled
her pockets with
in a circle on her kitchen table
and lets the silt on them dry completely

before she looks at them
with clarity

She has made a shrine
for all the tadpoles
that have met their maker
in her quest for the recklessness
of hands
to have meaning

IV

A pause; it endured horribly.

—*F. Scott Fitzgerald*

Intermission

I didn't want to write a poem today
but I am because that's what I do

I make the word *fuck* sound pretty

a thistle that is technically a daisy
and it's alluring like one
but it's still a goddamned weed at the core of things

I write metaphors about depression

and similes that make anxiety sound less debilitating
because calling the ugly-crying I do before getting a pap smear

"something with tears that leave burn marks, but made from the
same stuff as oceans, so they're still lovely,"

dresses that shit in beauty it doesn't deserve

If everything is lovely
nothing is lovely
right?

That's how it's supposed to go.

Writing is how I survive and poetry is how I make the survival
bearable

This poem is making my mouth taste bitter
as though I've just chewed up bay leaves
and I'm letting them congeal with the spit on my tongue
before I swallow

I wanted to write a poem about teenage infinity
and how sitting with my thigh touching my girlfriend's

heals the trauma I have from being undiagnosed with Autism until I
was already about to graduate high school
but instead I'm writing this

This is nothing
but it's also something

and it's something that I desperately needed

so I won't erase it from the internet and leave it behind after I talk
about it with my therapist next week

like a kid leaving the friend they met on the playground
and will never see again

even though they could have been soulmates of some kind

Because this poem
is a poem
and it sort of sounds nice
and it is how I will survive
today

Overture

what if

what if
what if
what if

what if

what if

what if

what if

what if

what if

what if

what if

what if

                                                    mouthful of pink apple

what if
what if
what if
what if
what if
what if
what if
what if
what if

        Buddha

what if

what if

what if

                                                  Vermillion
what if
what if
what if
what if
what if
what if
what if
what if
what if
what if
what if
what if
what if
what if
what if
what if
what if
what if
what if
what if
what if
what if
what if
what if
what if
what if
what if

                                          The Bechdel Test
                                               ichor
                                      The Bust of Nefertiti

what if

what if

what if

apricity

what if

a lioness

bohemian
Ariadne
idiosyncratic

                                        G-d is an atheist

V

I like seeing people when they can't see me.

—Dodie Smith

without a will

Wholeness is not for me
I was born already excavated
anything of value was pilfered by a twin
who smothered their own organs
with the opals from my
liberated placenta

Soft Skills

I step on every sidewalk crack
with both feet
digging the heels of
my favorite boots
into the sprouting clover

The shoes are orange
and used to be glossy
but now they're the dull lead of a ticonderoga pencil
that has gotten used to the feeling
of being choked out by a third grader

it kind of feels good to them now—
they are thinking of trying out bondage sometime soon

I don't hate my mother

She only spanked me once
even though
I probably deserved it more than that

because I used to take a lot of pride
in the fact that I could
say the alphabet backwards

and I did it so often
I forgot how to recite it the normal way

My term papers always came back
shrouded in red ink
because my teachers had to stand in front of a mirror
to read what I'd written

So I don't hate my mother
I just hate

that at some point
it was no longer cute
that the only skill I possess
is being able to do something the wrong way

No one asks me about
the movies I've seen anymore

because I describe the final scene
before the plot line
and I had to stop buying frosting

after my physician told me that if I kept
eating the entire canister
while my cakes were in the oven

diabetes would become the only animal
I could feed from my hand

What happens if I pay my electric bill two weeks late?

I will let this goddamned cigarette
burn
because the romanticism
that is smoking cloves
inside my first apartment

helps me to keep my balance
while walking backwards
around the jewel-toned velvet
couch I got from a discounted
furniture store
despite the wasp sting

I experienced when my friends started
telling me I was *not like other*
girls after they saw it for the first time.

The kitchen smoke detector
is shot anyways
because I grew up with a gas stove.

Besides,
I only picked this place
on account of it having
exposed brick

and I liked the idea
of being able to feel its
roughness
when my neurodivergence
is making everything
much too loud.

Three days ago I met the woman
who lives across the hall from me.

She asked me if I ever catsit,
and I said I did
because it didn't seem to be an
appropriate time
to tell her
that I am creeped out
by cats who don't have tails

and I saw that Winifred
had been declawed,
and a vegan I went out with several times
after Joan Fontaine passed away
and the other students

from my class on Haitian-American
film history
were holding nightly midnight protests
over the xenophobic injustice
of the university paper
not using her given French surname
of de Beauvoir de Havilland
in their 1,500 word tribute to the actress,

once told me that declawed felines
are more prone to
inappropriate elimination.

#13

She keeps a bottle of mineral water with her at all times and
magnesium is starting to possess the scent of my adoration for the
mole on the grooves of her spine

\#14

I hope she never washes the stained smudge of Marilyn Monroe
matte pigment on her lips off the fringe of her wine glasses

#15

I don't know if she knows the peridot on her avant-garde ring is my birthstone but I'd like to presume that she does

Sad, also happy

Mental illness and hot-faced sobbing aren't pretty, but van Gogh paintings are. Wait—this wasn't meant to be romantic. Not like clementine peels on worn car flooring in a van driving lovers to the beach. Not like summer storms or women dressed in early afternoon sunlight or nirvana. Because panic attacks are worse for the continual beating of the heart than middle school slander or alarmingly high cholesterol ever could be. Depression feels like being held down by humidity so weighted that you can't get up to make a bowl of cereal even when starving. Being actually, literally obsessed with something obstructs your ability to swallow because of the knots that form in your throat when you're pretty sure that your twin sister's airplane will fail mid-flight if you don't count syllables in your head until they reach a product of five, and that's obviously ridiculous, but it might be true, so how many syllables are in *onomatopoeia*, goddammit that's six, quick, think of another word. Mania is divine until you've got five maxed-out credit cards and chlamydia from the hypersexuality caused by your last episode. The ability to write gorgeous soliloquies is not worth suicidal ideation being a bad roommate you can't get rid of. I would rather live in a world without *For Whom the Bell Tolls* than know that Hemingway was familiar with the act of keeping mouthwash on the bedside table because if you can't brush your teeth at least you won't have to sit in your morning breath all day.

I liked the old weatherman better

i've
already brushed
my teeth

but dentists aren't even real doctors
and
i'm going to
eat this pecan square regardless

because watching
late night television
with the sound off

is the type of mildness
that i've
been lacking
ever since i got too old to put a spoon underneath my pillow
when i want it to snow

Tapas

I would make a charcuterie board
out of bits of my dog's intestines
and green olives from a jar in the
back of my refrigerator
without you asking me to
if it meant that your hunger would be
satisfied

An Ode to My Menstrual Cycle

Period

end
of sentence

Because when my body bleeds
instead of adding a mobile
to the nursery in my womb
that is the end of my humanity
for the month

Because it doesn't matter
that my stomach is rounded
from the watermelon that I grew
after swallowing the seed

The garden
inside of my body

plentiful
with stems
stronger than a baby's hands
filling my ribcage
like if they someday reach
my mouth

they will taste the sun

The sweetness
of this fruit
is better than anything
my uterus could create
with its pebble-infested soil

Children
don't bring you water

they just take your blood
and your milk

and leave you

as less of a person
so that they can become one themselves

My belly may not be tough
in order to protect itself
from the kicking
of the thing I am growing

but at least when I am cut open
there will be a feast
instead of another mouth to feed

Rhubarb Galette

Today I was 18 for the last time and I felt someone else's touch that
was meant in a way that was both sexual and hushed-lullaby
delicate and I know now what it is like to drink a strawberry
milkshake in the only 24-hour diner for miles as that one song
whirs in your ears and it was wonderful and I don't want to forget it
but I probably will because everything seems significant right now

Mouths

It's hard to breathe
with someone else's
air dripping down your throat

but this air tastes like
lavender macarons

so I will suffocate

Reminiscent of Fourth Grade Art Class

I met her
when she was a painting

She was the loveliest
shape
in the work's collection

and

I've always liked
abstract art

Her hips
are crescent rolls

oven-flushed
and perfect for
the breaking of a fast

She is the color of
deserted corridor light

Not glowy

but
shining all the same

I ache to carve her figure
out of the canvas
so

I will sit on my hands
until the urge passes

Because who am I

to ravage a creation
far greater
than anything

I could do
with these crooked fingers

What color will you do next? (probably magenta again)

The first time I dyed my hair

I used galaxy colors

My hair became a universe

something that I made more attractive
instead of destroyed

I'd done the destroying thing already

The chop, off all your hair
stop taking your lexapro because you don't deserve the peace it
gives you
have your mom lock the steak knives

and kitchen scissors

somewhere you can't find them
because if you did
you'd be in shreds,
thing

Don't get me wrong—

this isn't an apology for those times

or to those times

Maybe it should be
but it's not

I got the butch lesbian haircut
before I knew I liked girls
because I thought that if I slowed the process

of turning my body
into nothing but the air that I so resented
continuing to breathe

then perhaps I would find a reason to stay
alive before I wasn't anymore

After my first-ever depressive episode
I had an iris tattooed onto my arm

The end of the second was when I dyed my hair for the first time

Now I have photos of me
with hair so many different colors
I might as well line them up
and look for a pot of gold at either end

This time
after the suicidal thoughts
were resigned to the cramped backseat
of my swerving hatchback brain

I started writing poetry again

Because when I kind of enjoy
being alive
I find myself becoming one of those

insufferable people
who believe that their life will mean
something
even after it's over
and therefore
we should somehow
make that meaning

pretty

like leaving poems and pink hair strands
for people to find

when you are truly

definitively

nothing

anymore

Generational Feminism

My grandmother smoked pot with Betty Friedan sometimes / my mama was a staff sergeant in the Feminist Porn Wars / I listened to Beyonce's *Lemonade* while becoming a #nastywoman on Twitter / 1 in 5 female-identifying people will experience completed or attempted sexual violence in their lifetime / what was once a political movement has become a prerequisite for existing without pronouns that imply masculinity / today is a fine day for a revolution

Jesus Would Be a Democrat

I'm thinking of going to the grocery store
where smirking conservatives
coerce verses from Leviticus into my palms
when I try to walk past them
to get my dry shampoo

and kissing my girlfriend in front of them
as an act of protest

I will show them

how our bodies fit together
so perfectly

if the embrace wasn't created
with the two of us in mind

why does my head fit in the curve
where her neck meets her shoulder
as if they were shaped from the same mold of clay
during our making?

If God didn't mean
for me to find such solace
in the place where my girlfriend
presses her hands on my back
when she holds me

how could He have made
such an incredible mistake

that I find that safety anyways?

Because

I refuse to believe
that our Creator didn't make dreams
just so that we can see
each other's faces
even when our eyes are closed

So if they
try to tell me
that our God didn't shape this love

then
I will prove

that there isn't a God

if
He
wasn't the one
who gave me the ability to hear
so that I can know the sound of my girlfriend's windchime laughter

Worth the 75 cents

found possessed antique baby dolls for sale at the flea market;
bought one for the ninth grade version of myself who didn't believe
in compulsive heterosexuality as I wrote my own obituary after the
baseball player in my creative writing class didn't notice my new
Sinead O'Connor haircut; god she could have used the help of the
devil back then

(a portion of) The Things Found While Deep Cleaning My Bathroom

1. A disposable toothbrush from before my vacant womb was weaponized and people still had bodily autonomy (aren't you supposed to replace those things every three to four months?)

2. A Gillette Venus razor that I hid in my medicine cabinet after my boyfriend told me during a commercial break from his precious *Mad Men* reruns that he wished I shaved my pubic hair but I still refuse to throw away because that shit is expensive (and my grandma may be right that someday soon I will stop acting like the gender-confused lesbians found in a docuseries on second-wave feminism)

3. The package of 3-ply toilet paper my mom bought me when she visited for a long weekend that is only disturbed following the times when I've ignored my lactose intolerance diagnosis and consumed an entire wheel of brie for dinner at 3:45 in the morning (when a Bipolar II depressive episode hits there is only so much Zoloft can do for a girl)

4. A dirty bathroom carpet from when I don't wash the bottoms of my feet in the shower (likely because I was in the midst of considering the infinite artistry of my sister's seventh grade diary entries)

5. Walls painted a color named after ripe tangerines because fuck my ominous landlord and his fucking security deposit (also there is an ache in my gut to have a sexual identity based around citrus fruit)

6. A copy of *Paradise Lost* that a beautiful girl lent to me before we made love four times on her dorm room Twin XL in April, 2007 (sometimes when I am painting a jar of apple butter using the chiaroscuro effect I remember the way her saliva tasted like strawberry daiquiris)

I wish I hadn't already thrown away the box with the preheating temperature on it

1:27 a.m. and shivering and here and kind of okay.

I've been called worse than a hysterical bitch

This is it

the last of my soundness
has
been
dissolved into marjoram
vapor

Another woman
lost to crazed bliss

after she was not spoken over

Again, and Again, and Again

Waking up somewhere warm

maybe inside a taxicab

Back against the window
heated by a Sunday morning

where the sun has been tricked
into holding the Earth in place
as it pirouettes
for little while longer

and the driver turned the meter off
hours ago

Your head aches
like it's just been dumped
by the boyfriend it will still be in love with
for two more excruciating months
before it realizes he was a narcissist
and donates the sweatshirt he left in its laundry basket
to a charity that seems ethical enough

You need to shower

and buy potatoes that don't have eyes
because eating a vegetable
that can see the glint of your butter knife
seems a little cruel

You are fucking alive
and you've caught more lightning bugs
than colds

and you can hear a baby laughing

Maybe you'll have kids someday
or at least get a goldfish

That would be nice

But for now
you are still here

and the still being here

is the thing that matters

www.ingramcontent.com/pod-product-compliance
Lightning Source LLC
Chambersburg PA
CBHW071200120626
46546CB00006B/2353